SECRETS OF THE ANIMAL WORLD

BIRDS
Masters of Flight

by Eulalia García
Illustrated by Gabriel Casadevall and Ali Garousi

Gareth Stevens Publishing
MILWAUKEE

For a free color catalog describing Gareth Stevens' list of high-quality books and
multimedia programs, call 1-800-542-2595 (USA) or 1-800-461-9120 (Canada).
Gareth Stevens Publishing's Fax: (414) 225-0377.
See our catalog, too, on the World Wide Web: http://gsinc.com

The editor would like to extend special thanks to Jan W. Rafert, Curator of Primates
and Small Mammals, Milwaukee County Zoo, Milwaukee, Wisconsin, for his kind
and professional help with the information in this book.

Library of Congress Cataloging-in-Publication Data

García, Eulalia.
    [Aves. English]
    Birds: masters of flight / by Eulalia García ; illustrated by Gabriel Casadevall
    and Ali Garousi.
        p. cm. – (Secrets of the animal world)
    Includes bibliographical references and index.
    Summary: Describes the physical characteristics and habits of birds, with
    an emphasis on how birds fly.
    ISBN 0-8368-1638-2 (lib. bdg.)
    1. Birds–Juvenile literature. [1. Birds.] I. Casadevall, Gabriel, ill.
    II. Garousi, Ali, ill. III. Title. IV. Series.
    QL676.2.G36513 1997
    598–dc21   97-13054

This North American edition first published in 1997 by
Gareth Stevens Publishing
1555 North RiverCenter Drive, Suite 201
Milwaukee, Wisconsin 53212 USA

This U.S. edition © 1997 by Gareth Stevens, Inc. Created with original © 1993
Ediciones Este, S.A., Barcelona, Spain. Additional end matter © 1997 by Gareth
Stevens, Inc.

Series editor: Patricia Lantier-Sampon
Editorial assistants: Diane Laska, Rita Reitci

Printed in the United States of America

1 2 3 4 5 6 7 8 9 01 00 99 98 97

CONTENTS

LORDS OF THE AIR

Birds are easy to identify. If an animal has wings, feathers, and a beak, it's a bird!

What is a bird?

A bird is a vertebrate that lays eggs to reproduce. Feathers cover most of its body, and it has two wings and two legs, which it uses for jumping, running, landing, taking off, or propelling itself through water. The bird also has a beak, or bill.

Since most birds can fly, they live all over our planet — on the high seas, in deserts and tropical rain forests, in the countryside, in caves, in the polar regions, and on every island in the world.

The pelican's unusual bill has a pouch for holding captured fish.

Bird flight

Airplanes need a long runway to take off and fly. A bird takes off by flapping its wings up and down very quickly.

In the air, the bird defies the force of gravity by beating its wings. Aircraft have powerful engines that move their propellers. When an aircraft comes in to land, the pilot lowers the undercarriage and reduces engine speed. Birds lower their legs and brake by holding their wings behind them and opening their tail to create resistance.

Birds land to settle on a branch or the ground and sometimes to pounce on prey.

Bird flight compared to an airplane. A bird takes off by simply jumping; a plane needs to reach a high speed to take off. A bird flaps its wings to climb; an airplane uses engines. A bird slows down to land by opening its wings and tail; a plane reverses the thrust of its engines and lowers the wing flaps.

Types of birds

There is enormous diversity among Earth's bird species; there are over 8,600 known species. These species have different bills, feet, and wings. They eat different foods and live in various habitats. For example, some birds, such as ducks, swans, and seagulls, have webbed feet to help them move through water. A duck's bill can filter water out but still keep the food. Some birds appear to walk on stilts, such as herons, and are referred to as waders because they spend a lot of their time

External differences, such as wings, bills, and feet, help distinguish various bird species.

GULL

SPARROW

BALD EAGLE

DUCK

MACAW

GREAT BLUE HERON

walking around in swamps and other watery environments.

It is easy to recognize birds of prey, such as eagles and owls, by their silhouette. They have large, broad wings that help the birds glide while searching for prey. They also have strong, hooked beaks and feet with sharp talons. Parrots have brightly colored feathers and beaks that can remove seeds from shells.

OWL

INSIDE A BIRD

Most birds are similar on the inside. For instance, all birds have air sacs that make them lighter in weight.

All birds also have highly developed muscles to move their wings. Their skeletons are lightweight because many of the bones are hollow — these are referred to as pneumatic bones.

EYES
Sight is the bird's most developed sense, much more than smell, for locating food from the air.

SYRINX, or VOCAL APPARATUS
A chamber inside the trachea that produces the sounds of a bird's song.

ESOPHAGUS

BEAK
Instead of teeth, birds have a beak. The beak's shape varies according to the bird species and its diet.

TRACHEA

CROP
A pouch at the front of the esophagus, which is used to store and moisten food.

STERNUM
This bone anchors the muscles that move the wings. It has a bladelike extension, called the keel, where the muscles attach.

BLOOD VESSELS

KEEL

INTES

LIVER

FEMUR
The bones of land animals are filled with marrow. The bird's longest bones, such as the femur, are hollow.

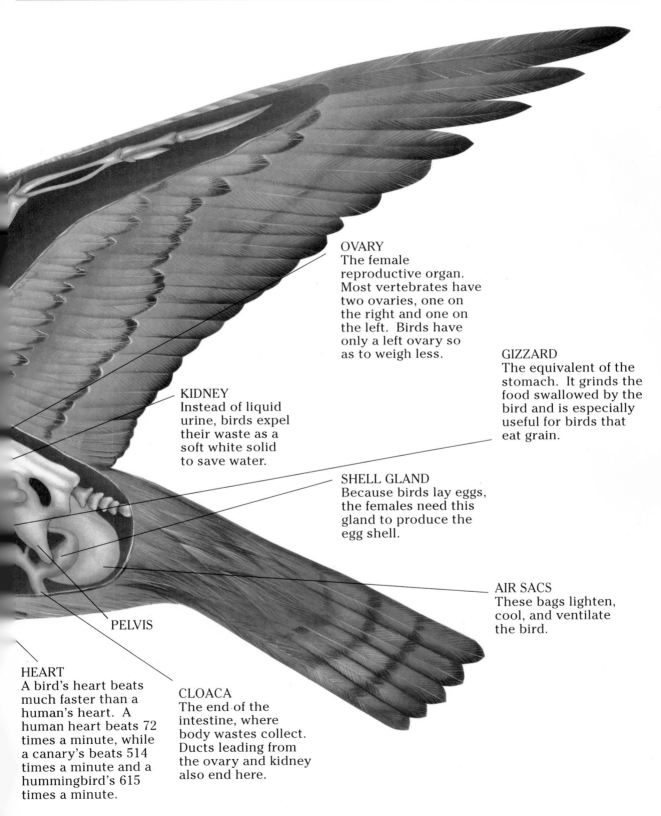

OVARY
The female reproductive organ. Most vertebrates have two ovaries, one on the right and one on the left. Birds have only a left ovary so as to weigh less.

GIZZARD
The equivalent of the stomach. It grinds the food swallowed by the bird and is especially useful for birds that eat grain.

KIDNEY
Instead of liquid urine, birds expel their waste as a soft white solid to save water.

SHELL GLAND
Because birds lay eggs, the females need this gland to produce the egg shell.

AIR SACS
These bags lighten, cool, and ventilate the bird.

PELVIS

HEART
A bird's heart beats much faster than a human's heart. A human heart beats 72 times a minute, while a canary's beats 514 times a minute and a hummingbird's 615 times a minute.

CLOACA
The end of the intestine, where body wastes collect. Ducts leading from the ovary and kidney also end here.

HOW DO BIRDS FLY?

Up into the air

Birds are light because their bones are hollow and they have air sacs connected to their lungs. This allows the bird to get off the ground and into the sky. Birds also have wings to help them fly, and they have an aerodynamic shape that enables them to speed through the air with ease.

The bird's wings are shaped like upside-down spoons. This shape helps the bird create a partial vacuum above the wings, where there is almost no air. At the same time, air accumulates below the wings, which the bird then uses to support itself in the sky. This flapping action keeps the bird in the air and propels it forward at the same time.

Flapping wings and a light body enable birds to take off. Once in the air, birds stroke their wings quickly to move forward.

Wings in flight curve their top surface, much like an airplane's wings, to help lift the bird.

that flightless birds exist?

Some birds cannot fly. The kiwi of New Zealand, for example, has wings, but they are so tiny they are almost invisible. Therefore, the bird cannot fly. Other flightless birds include ostriches and penguins. The ostrich is very large. An adult male can weigh over 350 pounds (160 kilograms).

This great weight is too much for the wings of the ostrich to lift in flight.

Feathers

Birds have between 1,300 and 12,000 feathers, according to their size. There are different kinds of feathers. Long, narrow feathers are used for flying. Some keep the birds warm, and others prevent water from reaching the skin. Tail feathers act as a rudder to maintain the animal's balance in flight. A layer of body contour feathers growing close together gives the bird a smooth look. Wings have the fewest feathers.

Feathers can also have decorative purposes. This male peafowl, or peacock, displays its magnificent back feathers to attract females (peahens).

Feathers vary in shape and size according to their use. They are used for staying warm, flying, showing off, and keeping balance.

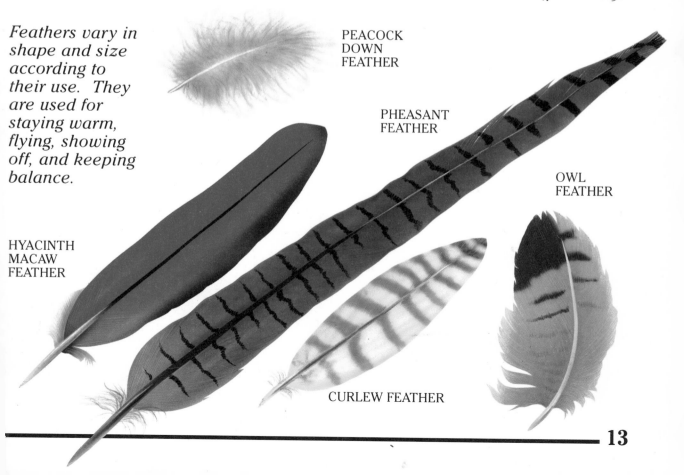

PEACOCK DOWN FEATHER

PHEASANT FEATHER

OWL FEATHER

HYACINTH MACAW FEATHER

CURLEW FEATHER

CONQUERING THE AIR

Flying techniques

Birds fly in two ways: by gliding with outstretched wings or by flapping them. To glide, the bird lets warm air currents take it up, and it returns down gradually.

The second type of flight consists of the bird flapping its wings very fast, which enables it to reach high speeds. Some birds can fly at speeds of 100 miles (160 kilometers) an hour.

Small birds do not usually glide. They just beat their wings rapidly.

Warm air rises, so birds use these air masses to gain height, which saves their energy.

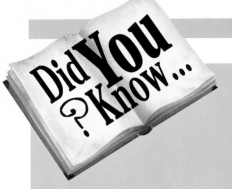
that some birds "sleep" while they are in the air?

Swifts can spend weeks in the air without landing. Their long, narrow wings enable them to fly high and fast. But their legs are weak. If they accidentally fall to the ground, they may be unable to fly again. Swifts are even said to "sleep" in the air, but they probably only take short naps. These birds can catch prey, eat, drink, and collect nesting materials while in flight.

Helicopters of the bird world

Some birds fly like helicopters. The hummingbird and certain kingfishers, for instance, hover in the air by flapping their wings quickly — between fifty and eighty times a second!

A kestrel can stay in the air motionless by holding its head up to the wind with its tail open while beating its wings. To catch prey, the bird closes its wings and dives head first toward the ground. These dives can reach speeds of 185 miles (300 km) an hour.

The hummingbird is the king of motionless flight. Its wings can beat over 80 times a second!

When the hovering kestrel sights prey, it snaps its wings to its body and dives downward. Just before reaching the ground, the kestrel spreads its wings to decrease its speed and opens its talons to seize its victim.

THE FIRST FLYERS

The first bird

Scientists believe the first bird was the Archaeopteryx. This bird had feathers and was about the size of a gull.

Archaeopteryx and the flying reptiles lived at the same time and place as the great dinosaurs.

Archaeopteryx looked very much like today's birds, in spite of some differences. It had three claws at the end of each wing. It also had a long tail, and its mouth was lined with more than forty teeth. None of today's birds have teeth.

Archaeopteryx climbed trees, from where it would launch itself and glide. It fed on insects it caught while gliding. Another flying creature, the pterosaur, also lived during this time. One toe on each front foot had developed into a long finger from which stretched its featherless skin wings.

Archaeopteryx not only looked like a bird, but a reptile, too, because of the many teeth in its jaws.

THE BIRD'S LIFE

Finding a mate

Birds mate during the warm months of the year. Each male has to find and attract a female. The male has many mating tricks: moving its wings, showing off its bright colors, jumping and walking in circles around a female, or offering food and nest-building materials. Some males also perform fantastic air tricks.

A male and female grebe form a pair. First they face each other, then they touch their breasts together and offer each other food as presents.

The male can do many things to attract a partner. He may dance in front of the female, give gifts, or show off the most striking part of its body.

Bird nests

After mating, the birds build a nest where the female will lay one, two, or more eggs.

Nests vary in size and shape. Some birds do not build a nest, but lay their eggs on the ground. Others build nests in tree trunks or in mounds of earth. Some nests are made of dry twigs laid together in the shape of a pot. More complex nests are made by intertwining twigs into nests with false entrances. Other nests are built under the roofs of houses, using mud mixed with the birds' own saliva.

Birds build nests to lay their eggs. They incubate the eggs by sitting on them until they hatch.

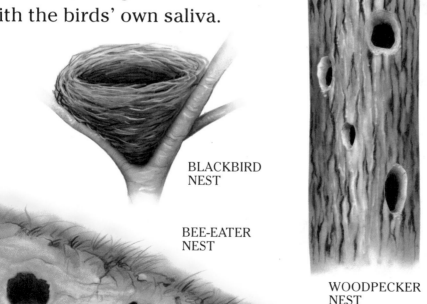

BLACKBIRD NEST

BEE-EATER NEST

WOODPECKER NEST

WEAVER NEST

Birds make nests in many shapes and sizes. One of the most original is the weaver's nest. This bird builds a false entrance on top of the real one to fool its enemies.

Packing their bags

Some birds are not always easy to observe. The swallow, for instance, can be seen only in the summer. It migrates in winter to a place where food is abundant.

Birds know when to leave as the days begin to get shorter in fall. This tells them it is time to migrate. A bird can fly between 1,550 and 1,864 miles (2,500 and 3,000 km) without stopping. Certain sea birds can cover even greater distances by gliding.

The albatross goes to dry land only to mate. Its nearly 13-foot (4-meter) wingspan allows it to cover long distances by flapping and gliding.

At night, birds use the stars to navigate. During the day, they use the position of the sun.

When birds migrate, they often fly in flocks. These wild geese are flying in V-shaped formation, with a bird in front as a guide.

that there are flying pirates?

Skua are "pirate" birds that feed by robbing prey caught by other birds. They attack other birds in the air, forcing them to release the prey. When a skua spies a bird carrying prey, it chases the bird until it catches up. Then the pirate bird pecks at the bird until it lets go of its food. The skua defends its nest against intruders by striking them on the head with its feet to scare them.

APPENDIX TO

SECRETS
OF THE
ANIMAL WORLD

BIRDS
Masters of Flight

BIRD SECRETS

▼ **A third eyelid.** Birds have three eyelids, two like humans have and a third that slides sideways independent of the other two.

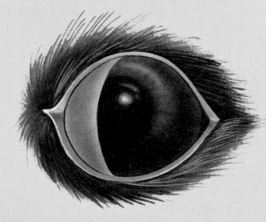

▼ **An insect trap.** The nightjar's mouth traps insects because of its enormous size and the hairs inside, which insects get stuck to as the bird flies through the air. The nightjar uses a special claw to keep these hairs clean.

▲ **Living and flying in caves.** The oilbird is a South American bird that lives in caves and feeds off the fruit of palms and other trees. The young of this species are so fat they weigh twice as much as their parents.

Longest feathers in the world. The bankiva rooster of Japan has the longest feathers in the world. Its tail feathers measure 35 feet (10.5 meters) in length.

▼ A pantry in the branches.

The shrike is a bird that usually spikes its prey (insects, small birds, or rodents) on the spines of bushes so that it can return for them later.

1. By flapping their wings, birds:
a) can rest while flying.
b) can build up speed.
c) can find a partner quickly.

2. How fast can the kestrel dive toward its prey?
a) 100 miles (161 km) per hour.
b) Over 75 miles (120 km) per hour.
c) 185 miles (300 km) per hour.

3. The first bird on Earth:
a) had a bill and feathers.
b) had feathers, but only on its wings.
c) had teeth and feathers.

4. Birds have the fewest feathers:
a) on their head.
b) on their body.
c) on their wings.

5. What are air sacs for?
a) To make the bird lightweight when it flies.
b) To float when swimming.
c) To hold in air while submerging.

6. How do birds know when it's time to migrate?
a) Food supplies run out.
b) Baby birds leave the nest.
c) The days become shorter.

The answers to BIRD SECRETS questions are on page 32.

GLOSSARY

abundant: plentiful; having a large amount.

accumulate: to gather, collect.

aerodynamic: having a streamlined shape that allows an object or animal to move easily through air or water.

air sac: a light pouch or bag in a bird's body that is filled with air.

birds of prey: birds, such as hawks, falcons, and owls, that hunt and eat other animals.

contour feathers: the medium-sized feathers that form the general covering of a bird and determine its external contour, or shape.

defy: to do something considered difficult or impossible.

distinguish: to see the differences among members of a group or class; to identify.

diversity: the condition of being different; a variety.

enable: to make possible or easy.

environment: the surroundings in which plants, animals, and other organisms live.

esophagus: the tube inside the body that connects the mouth to the stomach so food can pass into it; also called gullet.

external: on the outside or the outer surface.

femur: the leg bone closest to the body.

glide: to move slowly, quietly, and easily from one place to another, often without adding power.

gravity: Earth's attraction for objects in or on its surface.

habitat: the natural home of a plant or animal.

hover: to remain suspended in the same place while in the air.

incubate: to keep eggs warm, usually with body heat, so they will hatch.

intertwine: to twist or weave together.

intruder: someone or something that trespasses or enters an area without invitation or permission.

mate (v): to join together (animals) to produce young; to breed a male and a female.

migrate: to move from one place or climate to another, usually on a seasonal basis.

navigate: to find one's way from one place to another; to direct the course of a boat, plane, or craft of some sort.

pantry: a place where food is stored.

pirate: a robber on the high seas.

pneumatic: having air-filled cavities, such as air sacs and hollow bones.

polar: relating to those regions of Earth, centered around the North and South Poles, that are very cold and icy.

pouch: a part of the body that is like a bag.

pounce: to swoop upon and seize something; to make a sudden attack or approach.

prey: animals that are hunted, captured, and killed for food by other animals.

propel: to move something or to move oneself along in a forward direction.

propellers: a set of rotating blades used to move a ship or airplane.

recognize: to become aware of something that one has known or seen before.

reproduce: to mate, create offspring, and bear young.

reptiles: cold-blooded, egg-laying animals with an internal skeleton that have hornlike or scaly skin. Reptiles include snakes, turtles, and lizards. Pterosaurs were flying reptiles that lived in dinosaur times.

resistance: a force that slows down or opposes.

runway: a hard-surfaced strip of ground on a landing field for airplanes to take off or land.

saliva: the fluid produced in the mouth to keep it moist and to help in swallowing and digesting food.

silhouette: the outline of a body or object when the surface details cannot be easily seen.

species: animals or plants that are closely related and often similar in behavior and appearance. Members of the same species can breed together.

talons: the claws of a bird of prey.

thrust: a force pushing forward.

tropical: belonging to the tropics, or the region centered on the equator and lying between the Tropic of Cancer (23.5 degrees north of the equator) and the Tropic of Capricorn (23.5 degrees south of the equator). This region is typically very hot and humid.

undercarriage: the landing gear of an airplane.

vacuum: a space partly or entirely empty of everything, even air.

ventilate: to cause fresh air to circulate freely through a body or object.

vertebrate: any animal with a backbone of bony segments.

ACTIVITIES

◆ Feathers, with their patterns and colors, help identify birds and are beautiful to collect. You can make a feather "collection" of your own. Find some library books with color pictures of birds to use for reference. Draw a feather shape on thin cardboard and cut it out carefully. Place the cardboard shape on white paper and trace around it with pencil, making two or more rows of shapes. With crayons, markers, or watercolors, fill in each shape with the pattern of a different bird's feather. Write the bird's name next to its feather. You can use your collection to help identify birds you see outdoors.

◆ Many people keep birds as pets. Do some research at the library, talk to bird owners, or visit pet stores to find out what kinds of birds make good pets. How should pet birds be cared for? Do different birds require different kinds of care? Do they all eat the same kind of food? How can pet birds be kept healthy and free from pests? How do pet birds react to other animals in the house, such as cats or dogs?

MORE BOOKS TO READ

Animal Magic series. (Gareth Stevens)
Baby Birds. Secrets of the Animal World series. Eulalia García
    (Gareth Stevens)
Bird Watching for Kids. (NorthWord Press)
Crinkleroot's Guide to Knowing the Birds. J. Arnosky (Simon & Schuster)
Desert Birds. (Primer Publications)
Extremely Weird Birds. Sarah Lovett (John Muir)
The Feather Book. Karen O'Connor (Silver Burdett Press)
Jungle Birds. Anita Ganeri (Raintree Steck-Vaughn)
Owls. Animal Families series. Markus Kappeler (Gareth Stevens)
Passenger Pigeon. The Extinct Species Collection series.
    Graham Coleman (Gareth Stevens)

VIDEOS

Big Birds. (Rainbow Educational Media)
Birds and Birding. (Phoenix/BFA Film and Video)
Birds of Prey. (Rainbow Educational Media)
Land of the Birds. (Columbia Tristar Home Video)
Strange Birds. (Wood Knapp Video)

PLACES TO VISIT

Oklahoma City Zoo
2101 Northeast 50th Street
Oklahoma City, OK 73111

Granby Zoo
347 Bourget Street
Granby, Quebec J2G 1E8

Calgary Zoo
300 Zoo Road
Calgary, Alberta T2V 7E6

Indianapolis Zoo
White River State Park
1200 W. Washington Street
Indianapolis, IN 46222

**Royal Melbourne
    Zoological Gardens**
Elliot Avenue
Parkville, Victoria,
Australia 3052

Taronga Zoo
Bradleys Head Road
Mosman, NSW
Australia 2088

**Willowbrook Wildlife
    Reserve**
Christchurch
New Zealand

INDEX

**Answers to
BIRD SECRETS
questions:**
1. b
2. c
3. c
4. c
5. a
6. c